Catholic Things

A short poetry anthology

Edited by Janet McCann

Piddiddle Press

Piddiddle Press
1521 Foxfire Drive
College Station TX 77845

Published in the USA

ISBN 10: 0940807084
ISBN 14: 9780940807082

Dedication:

For all those we love
who have gone beyond us, to where
no Thing is needed

Catholic Things

Cover Art by **Linda Craig**

Catholic Things

The college chapel was still, cool. Everything I saw was wood—the sturdy pews, the altar, the walls, the window frames. I was alone, waiting for a friend. My first impression was that this would be a lovely place to come every day and pray. My friend did not turn up, so I sat in contemplation for a good while. I wanted to pray but found myself looking out the window, watching birds on a fence. For me this was not quite the right place. There were no things. Nothing to distract or interrupt—and yet I was not quite able to find my current of devotion.

Catholics need things, I thought, looking at the birds, watching them turn into metaphor. We need all sorts of things, concrete and immaterial, art, nature, symbols, places. These things are touchpoints between temporal and eternal, and there is a tactile quality to Catholicism—so many Thomases, we want to touch. Not to prove our faith, but to feel it. To take it in with the senses. So many nature poets are Catholic, in spirit if not in practice. Their poetry is immensely powerful because literal and metaphoric merge into one thing.

And what are these things? Everything. I think of Catholic art and the sacramental vision, the way of accessing the world so that its meaning and purpose come clear. The Catholic vision finds all kind of reflections and connections between time and eternity. Some are tiny—a woodpecker's tapping, a sudden rush of wind, carrying a small comfort to the observer. Others are immense and overwhelming, the true sacraments.

I remember that when we were growing up, my late husband's family had a box of broken sacramentals. I was not a Catholic then and I was fascinated by this wooden box with its broken rosaries, banged-up medals, and so forth. I wondered why they kept them, and yet the items seemed to have some trace of power left in them, and I picked up the beads and tarnished images with a bit of wonder.

When I became a Catholic the world seemed richer. Suddenly there were all sorts of conduits to the sacred that I had never imagined. Colors were symbolic. Daily acts acquired meaning. There were so many people and things in the world than I had believed. The thinginess of Catholicism was attractive. I had to work to avoid going too far into it, letting the things themselves dissolve in the meaning they carried.

I began to seek beautiful things that were charged with meaning. I saw art with different eyes—I had been looking for cleverness and innovation, envelope-pushing, boundary-crossing. But I traded in Jackson Pollock for Duccio. I went to remote places to gaze on paintings I had read about. The kind of faith that created that art is hard to find now, and even faith-based art now reflects a different world. Brother George Murphy, S.J., told me of a priest he knew who had started out as a skeptic but went to Italy to study art, and was converted. "He was brought to Christ by art," Brother George said.

I can see that. And still art and literature comes from our need for the holy.

These days are hard. On every side we see the visible absence of charity on every level. What do chaos, destructiveness, anarchy stand for? Nothing. Literally nothing. But as Christians we cannot believe that the world is unredeemable. So we look for these small and large epiphanies, these connections to the mystical. And they are there.

**

What is Catholic poetry?

Poetry written by Catholics? About Catholics? Expressing Catholic doctrines? What about attacking Catholic doctrines? My feeling is that it is so many things, and that there are so many categories of Catholic poets—some of which don't approve of others. I have to admit that I belong to most of them, different ones on different days. When I worked with a colleague on anthologies of Catholic poetry, we had many discussions about what it really was. And I came up with some overlapping types which, of course, are not limited to Catholics:

Devotional poetry, expressing belief and praise directly. May be Bible-based.

Sacramental-vision poetry, which looks at the world for those physical/spiritual connections between the temporal and the eternal.

Ethnic poetry about the Catholic lifestyle in particular groups.

Poems by saint-followers—I write a lot of these.

Poems ironical toward and critical about elements of the church— politically edged poems. Or poems that express disappointment in what is perceived as the Church's failure. May be apocalyptic.

Poems in search of faith—or renewed faith—God-seeking poems; poems of doubt and struggle.

Historical Catholic poems.

Nature poems which focus on the creator, Mary-Oliver style—also Gerard Manley Hopkins.

Poems that look at life events through a Catholic or even a simply metaphysical perspective—death, birth, change.

Poems that directly express Catholic doctrine with the intent to change behavior and/or belief.

Poems that just feel Catholic.

So why this project? No answer to that. I wanted to create a little anthology on the subject of Catholic Things, and decided to do so, for the benefit of those who enjoy such poems and the charity to which I consign any and all profits (??) I made no attempt to sort out the poems and paste them into any kind of categories, but just let the poems introduce and define themselves...

Alan Berecka

Beatification
     (St. George's, Utica, New York, 1971)

Her hand shot straight up. The missionary
stood stunned looking at the prim old lady
who sat straight-backed, front and center,
her arm raised solemnly like a witness
might before giving sworn testimony.

The priest had wandered from hundreds of pulpits
stood amongst a thousand strange flocks to launch
into his well-rehearsed patter by asking,
until now, the same rhetorical question,
Is there anyone here this morning who's a saint?

He took a hard look at the old woman
clad in black and dourness. He noticed
she wore hearing aids. *Ma'am perhaps you
didn't hear the question. I asked, is there...*
She cut him off, completed the sentence
anyone here a saint in a thick Lithuanian
accent. Her hand remained suspended.

Ma'am, do you know what a saint is?
She pointed to the statues on the side altars—
St. Jude and St. Anne. *Do you know saints
must work miracles, three of them, at least?*
Undaunted she replied, *I know this. I tell you.
I left old country by myself when just fifteen,
got into America, found job, and then husband.
We bought house. I gave birth to three strong sons.
My rosary and me prayed each one through
world war. Is this enough or do you want more?*

The priest, who slowly burned into the shade
of vestments at Pentecost, rebuffed the woman
saying, *Ma'am, indeed you've led a laudable life,
but the idea these common events are miracles,
I find laughable, after all, we can't all be saints.*
Her hand aloft she asked, *Then why are we here?*

Alan Berecka

Momma Tried

Riding home from mass
in the back seat next
to my sister, I turned
to her, a pink candy wafer
between my forefinger
and thumb. I said, *The body
of Necco.* She smiled,
offered her tongue.

Slap!

My ear rung—burned.
My face blistered red.
Our mother, the nice one,
was screaming in the bottom
of a well through stars,
*You've gone too far!
The sacred is no joke.*
My sister's jaw dropped.

This Sunday our priest
low balled the number
of communion wafers
only to be confronted
with an overflow crowd.
He quickly began splitting
each Eucharist into ever smaller
shares until we in the back pew
crowd arrived to receive an ort
of Jesus. Back on our kneeler,
I whispered to my wife, *Body of Christ
my ass. I think I got a big toe.*

She laughed. I flinched.

David Brunton

Incarnation

(Contemplation upon Dante Gabriel Rossetti's *Ecce Ancilla Domini*)

Before Gabriel the befuddled maiden
Supine, while in her countenance resolve
Fastens into the eyes, settles into the face now firm
For her fearful and unknown destiny:
Fiat mihi secundum verbum tuum

From the placental flow now Mystery forms,
Within the sanctified cocoon His life feeds: *Mater Dei*
The gurgling bruits of heartbeat, the protein flood,
The pulsed cells, purpled with oxygen, feed the flesh
Anxious to its mission

Tabernacled now in our frame of frailty
The ancient Logos mortalized, sown as creature
Condescending into our flawed and hellish place,
Vere Deum transmogrified, cast now as man
As birthed from Eden's soil

Fecund fluids creating Him who created her
As the purposed form takes shape:
He takes on flesh, that it might be bruised
He takes on visage that it might be struck
Blood, to be spilled as ransom

And His heart, that it might be pierced
As the sword of grief pierced hers:
Ecce Ancilla Domini

David Brunton

Two Fishes

so he blessed and broke the fishes
sent them forth to the five thousand
and does anybody wonder of the mechanics
did that first hungry hand grab

a chunk of one and another appeared
out of nothingness or did the baskets
come already overflowing or fall like manna
and that hungry hand grasped a handful

and a couple of loaves to boot five
thousand hands, God's food to them
two broken fishes, still remaining, I'd think
when the leftover buckets were gathered

so the skeptic says to me how could it be his
body parsed out to the twelve as he remains
intact on the cushioned floor, lifts the cup
and fills it with his blood as yet unspilled?

I say do you not know of the two fishes
and his power to feed a field, a world,
of fasting bodies and famished souls
if fish out of nothing, himself from himself

is an easier challenge

William Bedford Clark

St. John Fisher: Bishop and Martyr

"Well-met, Reverend Sir. We may soon make merry in Heaven."

"Verily, for we have entered through a strait gate."

---- Thomas More meets John Fisher in the Tower

The head was off before the crimson hat
Arrived – Oh John, who fished for men, knaves say
You knew how death leaned close and it was that
That nerved your stout resolve to bark a nay.

The head was off – but on the traitor's pike
Its grim and pinched façade grew ruddy young,
Aflush with Cana-wine. The headsman's strike
Recalled another John – the dance and song
Antipas called – so plain folk whispered loud
Along the bridge and in the cauldron streets.
Then Henry paused, but donned his purple shroud
To churn again between infernal sheets.

At this late date, staunch John, Rochester's Rock,
Pray hard for shepherds who sell short the flock.
Your Tudor peers feared fire, the rough-hewn block:
They might have held against progressive talk.

William Bedford Clark

Their Last Pagan Easter

Late snow across the southern plains
Laid waste their Spring Break westering.
Retreating east, they chose toward dark
A needful knotty-pine motel
Along State Line in Arkansas.

Back in the day, one knew the drill:
She gloved her hands to hide the ring
That wasn't there; he gave false names.
Then they, the sole guests registered,
Were honored with a gift to mark
That date they'd managed to suppress.

Their hostess – old, half-blind, blue-eyed,
Godmotherly – handed the girl
A clutch of lilies, white and gold,
Salvaged from Easter services
At Zion Freewill Baptist Church.

Her son, past middle-age, flesh slack
On heavy frame, stood counter-side;
His slanted gaze was cold – and wise.
He pulled the key to Cabin 8,
Which proved a musty, umbrous space.

They'd thought to spend that night like they'd
Spent Lent, in carnal Mardi Gras,
But something came between them in
That narrow bed. They rushed to leave
Before first light – turned south toward home –
Quite unaware they traveled now
On two diverging paths to Rome.

William Bedford Clark

The Reluctant Thomist Teaches PHIL 101

> . . . on our very hearths and in our gardens
> the infernal cat plays with the panting mouse,
> or holds the hot bird fluttering in her jaws.
>
> – William James

Bear's hot breath on the hiker's face –
Shark-slice along the diver's thigh –
Bee-barb deep in the baby's thumb –
Worm-crawl across the inner eye:

> *was Wordsworth wrong*
> *and Darwin right?*

Storm-surge fouling the harborside –
Long bridges swaying way to stress –
Dark-tailed twisters abducting herds –
The Big One roiling up the West:

> *was Leibnitz wrong*
> *and Voltaire right?*

Live-In Boyfriend Abuses Child –
Veiled Girl Trips Bomb in Marketplace –
Judge Says No to Hydration Tube –
Clerk Disappears Without a Trace –

was Rousseau wrong
and Calvin right?

Is Evil deprivation of the Good?
I'd like to think that's so, if I but could.

David Craig

The Scorners Outside Us

They expected us to be better people. To queue up for a ball—
to have read the damned book! They really don't ask for much,
after all, just the sun, rain, some purple clover.

But I can never make my tie come straight, and that's
just the first stanza. The next thing is the car I drive,
my side of the road. (And Keats was too poor, too short.)

This is what it means to wake up in the morning any more.
It's the white noise that gets us out the door,
the piazza in Florence, Dante's mask, his font.

The Etruscans had the same problem, except for them,
it was small red flowers. They came out everywhere, along
foundations, in the living room. Foreigners laughed.

But everything is praise. Much that is, all that will be.
And the road doesn't finish. The blue sky is not king.
It is a glorious stepstool. That's why we write these poems.

The world is a flag, waving us as we wave it.
(Make sure no one falls off!) Jesus does make laws,
but only for the Etruscans who are so slow of heart.

David Craig

The Pope's Longing

He longs for dogs, having the run of the place.
He longs for the white mountains of his childhood, his nurse
who used to call him by a thousand other names.

Sometimes when he sips his coffee, he longs for the stark,
pocked and ravaged moon high above the pampas,
for the woman at the newsstand, her gritty takes on the
neighborhood.

The darkness falling over Rome cannot save him.
John the Twenty-Third still walks night halls.
A Titian cries with eleven Apostles in the basement.

The lightbulb clicks on, and he washes his hands yet again.
The echo of a door knob turning is only that.
Jesus will have to save this day as well.

Flamingoes rise up as one in some tropical place.
In another, a bomb explodes, even as a fine
briefcase snap shut, someone whispers on his right.

He struggles to be small enough, to get out of the way,
as pigeons flutter the circle that's Peter's Square.
He will never understand the ways of God.

David Craig

Out There

We were the neighborhood sore thumb,
the Catholic menace in gray shingle,
farmhouse to their suburban tracts.
My parents must have seemed communist in kids,
our house facing the main road, backyard,
more dirt than grass, open to their side street.
My brothers, to the chagrin of our neighbors,
built a fort in the oldest tree out back,
would push kids out of it, flip darts at calves
as they ran away. Protestant mothers
were horrified, Juniors, in Bermudas, at bay.

But we had both the plum and apple trees,
and those rebellious Protestants could climb
as high as any of us, to the crack of branches,
splitting bark, the fibrous wood flower splintering,
as we fished far out for green globes.
The clouds were up there, the sun, and all of us
on bikes after, to Gunning's for a swim.

Sure my brothers were crazy: Tim chasing Pat
with an ax. Minor police investigations.
And my father, limping on his high shoe,
'55 Ford-red wagon parked on the street.
Dressed like the blue-collar worker he was,
he'd play games with us in the back yard,
his one skinny polio arm, the underneath part
flapping as he moved out there,
the whole neighborhood to see.

Sybil Estess

Labyrinth, Fourteen Ways

When you walk it

you are seldom lonely.

When you walk it,

there are other people

on their own path. When

you walk with another,

you pay attention

to your path--not to theirs.

When you walk with care,

the two of you never collide.

When you walk it,

you must look and listen.

When you walk it,

you are by yourself--but not.

When you walk it

you get to a still-point.

When you get there,

you are not finished yet.

When you arrive,

and rest at the rose center,

you must exit as

Christ did: down the Mount

of Transfiguration.

To Jerusalem.

When you walk it, you

have to trek and work your way out.

Sybil Estess

Villa de Matel, Houston

At twilight an old nun paddles toward me
in her life-jacket, bright blue. I am so
quiet for the day at the retreat house.

Here, women believe things are possible,
even the impossible....They start with
exercise on summer evenings before

any dim night of the soul. The lady
says she is glad I have come for the day
to pray—although I'm protestant. She says

she assumes never again will there be
a convent as big as this one. For God,
she claims, is a spirit of change. Acres

here in the city are gardened, Eden-
like. Geraniums, hibiscus, fountains,
grottos, paths wind everywhere to statues

of the Virgin. The nun says she thanks Christ
all the time for Vatican II, floating folks
like her and me together. She works with

cancer patients, sees that the Lord never
notices what denomination any suffering
woman is, or dying man...

She hastens to say that parents should not
wait for the church, but teach God themselves
to their own. She whispers this between breaths,

while stroking. It is good, I say, she does
not swim alone. At her age, a body-
buoy—Blue as Mary's mantilla—brings

brilliant company. Near fifty, I try
laps when my aged confidante leaves me
in indigo silence. I will to believe.

John Finlay

A Prayer to the Paraclete

God the Spirit, inspire
Our soul's and body's life
With purifying fire.
Let not quick sin be rife.

Cleanse the barren mind
Of crudities and lies
That it, at last, may find
Truth which fructifies.

Let charity fuse whole
The fractured, wounded will,
Each movement of the soul
To God Who makes us still.

And never let despair
Defeat the Father's plan:
Christ gives us God to share
In His shed blood as man.

John Finlay

The Autobiography of a Benedictine

I teach logic to would-be priests,
The subtlest training of the Schools.
A keen, well-bred old hound unleasht,
I track down fallacies of fools.

I read dry Horace, drink wine deep,
Though never yet to drown my wits.
Old Cock is cooked, and so I sleep
Long nights unshaken by his fits.

I feel at ease here on this earth
And love the dogma of God's flesh.
Why should we see a poisonous dearth
In what God still creates afresh?

That sun-struck Porch of Solomon,
Those eunuchs of the maddening groan
Who insult reason, who would stun
Our souls with God, I leave alone.

Athena's grove, its tempered air,
The autumn sun on her olive trees—
I thrive and bead my thankful prayer
To reason's source for clarities.

Our mind is not some Virgil cursed
To go back down to painful shades.
Faith dies itself and is dispersed
In minds the deathless Word pervades.

John Finlay

A Prayer to the Father

Death is not far from me. At times I crave
The peace I think that it will bring. Be brave,
I tell myself, for soon your pain will cease.
But terror still obtains when our long lease
On life ends at last. Body and soul,
Which fused together should make up one whole,
Suffer deprived as they are wrenched apart.
O God of love and power, hold still my heart
When death, that ancient, awful fact appears;
Preserve my mind from all deranging fears,
And let me offer up my reason free
And where I thought, there see Thee perfectly.

—Spring 1990

Andrew Laurence Graney

After Viewing my Cousin's Body

I kneeled at a pew and prayed,
Our Father... Hail Mary... Glory Be...
as if the prayers' words were the only words
I knew, hoping they would stifle
sniffles, drown wails, raze grief.

The line of mourners started to salamander
to the door, and, to my disbelief, I heard *thy kingdom
come* become my observation. Amid the righteous
anger, the balling, the stuffing balled up tissues
in pockets, you revealed to me a pocket

of, (and I'm almost ashamed to say it now),
your joy, (I feel sick), your communion.
The stained glass windows darkened
as if to offer me their light, and the pew,
the prayers, the sniffles and wails,

the line stretching from altar to exit,
the altar and the exit, it was yours, all yours.
Lord, I was not worthy, but you entered
under the roof of my mouth, and every syllable
filled me as if I ate a cloud and killed the rain.

Andrew Laurence Graney

Happy Hour

But she wouldn't buy my story, he said of his doctor
as he waved down the barkeep for another
Dark & Stormy, *so I'm writing my own script.*

When I asked him his story, how he hurt
his back, he replied, *heavy lifting.* A non-answer
that answered all I needed to know, said all

he didn't want to explain of his complaint
having nothing, or little, to do with physical
pain, and yet everything to do with an ache

that no doubt made it difficult for him to leave his bed,
but to serve the doctor that dish? He was so far gone
I could have contacted scientists everywhere

to let them know, yes, life indeed exists on other planets.
And who knows, he might well have enjoyed that joke.
It might have given him a moment's relief, or

it might have acted like CPR to his anger. He didn't need
to feel more broken; he needed a break. God, gulp-silent,
what did I offer, down which path did I help him travel?

Andrew Laurence Graney

**Failing to Concentrate as I Try to Read,
I Set the Book on my Desk and Close my Eyes**

The central air kicks on again,
settles. Garbage truck brakes
squeak. A cardinal seems to
copycat. Wonderful. Landing
in or leaving Philadelphia, a plane
drapes its long noise over north Wilmington.
Then, silence. Like an argument
ended, like being stunned
by a present, like the infinite
listening to the rest of creation.

Kathleen Hart

The Last Day

Sir Walter Raleigh, who teaches us
that you can write *The History of the World*
and still be executed, wrote to his wife
the night before his beheading: *It is also
high time that I separate my thoughts
from the world.* Others won't realize
what is going to happen, like the Death Row
inmate who left the pecan pie from his last
meal behind because he wanted to save
it for later.

But even as we speak, today's weather system
is diminishing and blowing itself out to sea,
and the very universe is expanding and pulling
itself apart.

I hope that my coffee in bed with my newspaper
won't be rushed, and that I happen to glance out
the window the moment dark becomes light.
In this version of my last day, I will see
the dogwoods in full bloom, even if they don't
appear to be, and they will lift me up and take
me into their confidence.

Kathleen Hart

Natural Causes
 -a case from 48Hours: Missing Persons

Not a suicide. You just knew you were going to die
that day. And I imagine that, at first, you wanted to believe
that saying the facts – cancer, breakthrough pain –
didn't make them so. At first, the facts weren't in your favor,
and every anxiety was justified as they woke you up at 3 a. m.
with too much night to swallow.

Then you knew you didn't reside in the realm of hope to live
anymore, and the time to anticipate, head off, and reckon with
them was over. You knew, the facts would get you nowhere.

So you let them slip back through gaps in the wall, back alleys,
and shortcuts until, after months, they finally just stood up and
walked away from the conversation, leaving you free to wander.
Which is how your name was broadcast as an endangered adult.

Since death is supposed to be a journey, you put your overcoat on,
took your last dose of medication, and left your pill bottle and keys
on the kitchen table. When you looked at the sky, the day
mercifully
refused to look different from any other. You went to the railroad
station and bought a ticket for the last stop before Illinois
becomes Wisconsin.

You were found the next day lying in the woods beside the tracks
where the trains turn around to go back to Chicago. The coroner
reported that you just went to sleep and didn't wake up.

I see you stretched out on the leaves and murmuring to your
daughter,
opening yourself to the realm of possibility, opening yourself to the
stars and
their constellations, becoming one with them, becoming one with
your maker.

Leo Luke Marcello

Afternoon on the Creole Nature Trail
     elegy for Father Gerry Maloney

"Life cannot be saved! It can only be spent!. . . So, study, not to
save, but to spend. To make valuable by dealing with valuable
things in the time I have. It will pass soon. Like an afternoon.
Years are as days and are over. So live each one on its own terms,
on the best terms possible. And then, die, and go to God! Not
Androcles' 'sweet bye and bye.' That is saccharine and superficial.
But in the Trinity."
     (journal entry a few days before his sudden death)

We die on islands far apart,
some of us disappearing as suddenly
as a warm breeze crossing prairie
in search of open water.

You and I stood on a platform once,
leaning against the raw-wood railing,
perusing the wide flat land stretching
to the Gulf. Our voices, tangling
with the wind seemed a steady hum
under its whip beating our faces,
bellowing our shirts, and then
disappearing into the tall grasses.

We were comparing notes on the horizon.
I was on my way into the seminary
where you'd already been.
You were vacationing in my territory
far away from your own Australia
and another hemisphere.

We descended, retracing the trail.
Alligators were sunning themselves,
inert, not yet fully awake to another
mating season. We walked close enough
to feel their sleeping.

I did not know we'd never meet again.
You collapsed suddenly at home in Fiji,
at peace your last words proclaim:

"Life cannot be saved!
It will pass soon.
Like an afternoon.
It can only be spent."

I stand alone on a platform, Gerry.
The seasons have come around again.
Already there is another generation
sunning itself in the wild grasses,
waiting to be awakened once more.

Janet McCann

Life List

in memory of S. A.

My friend the scholar-birdwatcher
is dying, after a quiet regular life
of Milton and birds, and if I could

imagine him a farewell, it would be this:
to look out into the small yard
he tended for forty years, to where

he placed the bird houses, the martin
house and the hummingbird feeder,
just in time to see a sweep of air

curve in and take form, the great arctic gyrfalcon
not on his life list, there on the sill,
to be recognized by beak, feathers and pinions

and final knowledge, Adam's homecoming
after the story's end, better than Eden.
May he have in his hand a feather, that his wife

might know where he has gone.

Janet McCann

Clare's Grate

behind glass in her Assisi church
near the immense and intricate white dress
she made for a big nun, west of the slippers
carefully sewn for the marked and dying Francis,

is the square of iron scrollwork with its door
she could open to see, to be seen.
Through the scrolling she would seem a shadow
a series of graceful motions, talking ghost,

but if she chose to open, on those days
her visage would be fully visible
to seekers. Did the hinges creak, complain
as she opened to traveling monks, young women

looking for shelter, their angry fathers
who came after them, popes and bishops?
How often did she open it to Francis,
did she ever reach her hand through to touch his?

--that metal grate, faintly glimmering
in its glass case, curlicues of hammered iron
(that in this muted light looks more like silver)
for her to sit behind, lean toward, throw open.

Paul McCann

Understanding Picasso

"Research reveals Picasso's wish to die in communion with the Church"

Pablo collects pebbles.
Mounds of them
and processes
splitting those from mere rocks
rigid standards
that stones must acquiesce to.

Has it been skipped along stagnant pools
or cast forward from the center of the earth
to be cooled and polished under glorious sun.
Does it speak?
Some have been cut by rain into
six carat granite displacing hollow time
and are mere stones no more but epic,
leaving Pablo to reflect sadly that
the destiny of men lies in rocks.

Reminding Patience
Slighting Courage
Pablo spreads these before him
On the breezeway and over the garden
Terra Firma Earth Quarry
For Pablo will not walk on pebbles
of broken glass
but only on the very tears of God.
Everything is real
with eyes open and pure
a melancholy man already pale
under September blue
is spanked by sunlight
and adds the proper shading.

Paul McCann

The Accidental Catholic

I want something easier than the sandy loam
Beneath bent oaks that yields so little to the child's shovel.
With no yard, I had suggested the dumpster
to a five year old girl who, in truth, was indifferent
to the rabbit when it was alive.
     But rabbits were her favorite characters,
Rabbits, the iconography of her buttons,
Rabbits, the soft flour of her bedtime.
     We have no yard and though
the dumpster waits patiently as I drive by,
the promises between fathers and daughters
are sacred things.
     So I filched a yard passed the playground
in the wooded park where her child hood imagination
saw lurking dragons and singing knights,
passed the turtles leisurely
swimming in a stew of bread crumbs.
Beach toys for burial, the plastic of two
Have already snapped between the stubborn roots.
Scratch and scratch again in April sweat
exhausted before a shallow grave,
the dead receive their rights.

     Let us be the child again
weeping on Easter morning.
Dogs will pause here to impatient owners
and sniff earnestly at the seashell cross.
     Let us be the rabbit
nibbling gifted kale.
Owners with wrinkled noses will coax
the leash back into the business of the living.
     Let us the be the father
burdened with his promises.
The stolen grave makes interest
     On my redemption.
     And let us always stray
before our next confession.

David Middleton

Vigils

a north Louisianian looks south

January 6, Epiphany and the first day of Mardi Gras

The quiet alone is holy and enough
So long as night still darkens into dawn
And fallen starlight rises from a lawn
Whose snowflakes twinkle deep in matter's stuff.

And on this night when hope and fear grew calm
The Wise Men knelt where Child and Mother were
With gifts of gold and frankincense and myrrh
For king and god, for soul and body's balm.

And as the words of Matthew draw me in
Once more to where the heart and mind are one
Though history and myth have come undone
In these late days when faith itself is sin

I think how many winters just the same
Revels of music, food, drink, dance, and sex
Have ruled with Orpheus, Comus, Bacchus, Rex—
Those passing kings great crowds loudly acclaim.

Now stars of Hollywood outshine the Star
With glittering gifts all wise men would disdain
Though thousands wait for throws in dark and rain,
Not Gaspar, Melchior, and Balthazar.

And so Old Adam still will have his day
As celebrant at feasts some people keep
For flesh and blood that never wake from sleep,
This bread and wine of human show and play.

Yet now and then forever in the fields
Of space and time whose carnivals will end
Shepherds abide through night to watch and tend
Till Wise Men come to know and knowledge yields.

David Middleton

Headmaster, Mother, Son

--at a parochial prep school

A mother and the tired headmaster sat
Relaxing in his office while her son
Was being interviewed, but then their chat
Grew tense once her hard questions had begun.

The mother said, "Headmaster, let's be clear.
This prep school is elite and rigorous,
Expensive, too, so if our son comes here
What's in it in the end for him and us?

Will he succeed in business, politics,
Make good connections, have his name put down
Before some flashy whiz kid's from the sticks
For Princeton, Harvard, Yale, Cornell, or Brown?"

"Yes, Madam, if your boy is bright enough
To be admitted, works hard, he'll do well
Because our old curriculum is tough,
But that is not an end on which we dwell."

"Then what," quipped she, "is your primary goal?"
(Miffed and bewildered, letting out her breath);
And he, "To tend to body, mind, and soul
And to prepare him, in a word, for death."

Kay Mullen

Hidden Mystics
Retreat at a Monastery

This monastic chapel reflects a medley
of tenets. No figures of saints
       or rose design wedges,

only spaces and shapes of inherent mystics
lie hidden there. The Tao's praise of silence
       flows through ivory tint,

radical abandon like wind through hollows
       as the ordinary earns
honor in a vast empty place of no-knowing.

A Zen lamp of liberation shines. With mystical
acumen, Christ speaks in triangular shapes, all
       loving presence,

lotus of the heart. A path of presence
       surrenders to fire
a blue background, Islam's flame,
a square panel in a gold vessel.

Through choral hue, Allah appeals for peace.
The Dharma sits in a triangular pane

at the edge of a sea wall, ponders the waves,
       a trickle of water down
from the mountain where Santor's stream

has no end. So many enduring rivers
surge through leaded glass, so many homes,
       so many beliefs flowing through light.

Kay Mullen

In Bas-relief

1

On Novena nights, my childhood friend and I kneel
in the same pew at St. Ann's. Across the aisle,
a stained glass window opens to sultry summer air.
Above, a woman sits between stone columns
outside an upstairs window. She presses her smallest
finger against her lip, thumb on her chin bone, elbow
in her left palm. This third station-of-the-cross
unnerves me every Friday night. I see only
indifference in her pose, her eyes as she stares
beyond the scene below as if atrocities were trivial,
as if the stricken man bearing wood beams
did not create a crime against the world.

I wonder why she doesn't join the weeping women,
stand beside the brave, bloody her hands, chance life.
All I see is stone.

2

Years pass and now she speaks to me from the same
sill. *You question my intent, see only from your side.*
Here on this ledge soldier eyes follow my every move.
I pretend dispassion for this torn man in the screaming
below whose last meal I served a night ago. I forgive your
judgments. The day will come for me to answer—and for you.

Stella Nesanovich

Following Mary in Passion Week

I. The Seder

Only the tattered disciples,
the meal unsettled by questions
of coming betrayal: her son,
the servant to servants.

She knows about serving. Waiting
in shadows, she ponders
his kneeling to wash their feet.

She remembers how he carried
wood for his father, learned
to return the beetle to its mate,
let the lizard go off to the desert.
Once a beggar stopped for drink.
Jesus lifted the cup. Sun sparkled
from the well water as the man
stood speechless, sand-crusted,
soiled kerchief at his neck.

II. The Way of the Cross

She hears the whispers, sees
the glances of the Sanhedrin
and grieves the pronouncement
of Pilate, her child stripped
and whipped. Along the path
to Golgotha, she watches him fall,
his struggle with the beam
over lacerated shoulders.
Weakened, barely clothed
in purple, he staggers
like some debauched king,
his head bound with thorns
and so blooded, he is blinded
while strangers shout for him
to hurry and hecklers spit.

III. *Stabat Mater*

She wants to wipe his face,
take him to her breast, the child
who brought her stones
from the garden, pebbles
the color of his eyes. The sky
is too low, and the earth rattles
as if to throw off shackles.

He endures the torture,
this crime of jealous men,
frightened for their positions,
power bestowed by Rome.
That Jesus would doubt—
what agony does! And the finish:
the sun hidden, the earth dark,
seismic, trembling beneath them.

She waits with Martha and Mary
for the soldier's pronouncement,
for her son's broken body.
She will wrap his feet and legs,
prepare him for the garden tomb
Joseph of Arimathea has given.

Nicodemus comes to help,
brings myrrh and aloes
in alabaster jars. She keens
silently, caresses Jesus'
weeping flesh, rocks him
as she did when a babe.

Lois Roma-Deeley

Given Notice

Just yesterday I saw a man walking on his knees
down the aisle of St. Thomas the Apostle.
And you would think he'd be embarrassed,
having, alongside him, his upright wife
looking down into his bearded face
like she was heeling her shaggy dog.
But no.
With both arms lifted in prayer and
with his hands folded, lightly, around the wood rosary
which fell from his fingers in a graceful "U,"
the beads swinging in the air with slow and delicate movements,
he stopped.
When the man raised his eyes
to the gilt ceiling above our heads,
my eyes followed his—

past the gold leaf angels on the wall
to the dome where a crown of blue stars
surrounds the Virgin's head and
there, on her lap, the baby Jesus, smiling
at the man who is smiling back at him.
I have often wished for this kind of faith—
pure and unyielding as a force of nature

like a tornado sucking up trees, trucks, telephone poles, pigs,
whole towns—you name it—
to be taken with certainty, not pity,
into the funnel cloud which twists over ground.

Lois Roma-Deeley

The Dark Night Speaks to the Soul

after Psalm 88

Your prayers begin and end unanswered
as echoes in a whirlwind. You're shattered.
A tornado of fear has ripped away
your insight. Now going down and climbing
into a storm cellar, there's the moonlight
falling so unevenly across the staircase
of theoretical stone. And in this way
your heart can understand how an outbreak
of reason is not a whisper of unholy light—
the broken window through which your are afraid
to listen. Yet, like the madman with a bouquet
of tin cans, you'll rattle against the balustrades
until someone comes and tells you *it's all right...*
Who does not fear the face of unkind time?
the dark void your earth keeps talking to in space?
that utterance, a stillness, to keep you afraid?

Olympia Sibley

The Eleventh Virgin

I'm not even—really. And
I've got plenty of oil
purchased at unbelievably
low prices from a three-
handed merchant with a stall
in the mutant market.

But, I can't find my lamp.
Which is sad for several
reasons. It's a legacy
position, being a lamp bearing
virgin, and it's sad to lose
part of one's history even
if only dimly recalled.

I do remember the lamp. Could
identify it if I had to. I think
the numbers stamped
on its base are supposed to match
the ones tattooed on the nape
of my neck. (Why I don't
wear my hair up.)

Another reason it's sad I don't
have my lamp is that I was waiting
for someone or something
special (I assume) but I can't
exactly remember who or what
and maybe if I had the lamp
again, filled it with oil, trimmed
the wick, and set it on fire
it would trigger something
in my memory—but in a good
way—not like the ones who run
screaming or go catatonic
whenever the weather is just
a little bit off or ash blows
in from the East. I wonder

if the woman who used to
weave wicks is still alive.

Olympia Sibley

Day 42

Make me but a colander
in the kitchen of Your Kingdom.

Let me be hung
over a pearl counter
near a bath-sized sink.

Let the ringing laughter
of the better guests
buoy me from
the banquet hall.

Let me be grasped
by competent hands.

Let me never fall.

Let only good things
be poured into me.

Let the unnecessary
drain out of me.

Let me bear no more than
one ingredient at a time.

Let me be scoured clean
with copper-wire brushes
and chlorine bleach
if that's what it takes.

Let me shine.

Let me be bright blue
as a Spring robin's egg
but already broken
open.

Chuck Taylor

As You Face the End

Oh I have seen the suffering Christ
set in naves against so many Catholic walls,
black-bearded in the armor of a lonely pain

And so do I come to whisper in all ears,
to disturb the sorrowful voices

I bring soiled hands white, pink-tinged,
Flowers, and a promise--
the warm edge of sun
and rain in an early afternoon

My God, I whisper through flowers,
when this life is over you and I will
walk the sunlit fields

We will stop to cool our feet in waters

I will show you a rope and a willow.
Children will swing out over the waters.

Their laughter will be our faith

Chuck Taylor

Honors Class During Iraqi War, 2003

Young, blue eyed, and blond, she explains in the old
classroom, how he was elected leader
but he was actually chosen by
God and now he speaks and acts for our God.

Old, brown eyed, and white haired, he, in the chalk
dust day of war in History's Building,
asks if church-going democrats who get
elected president also speak and

act for God; ask if Hitler spoke and did
concentrating for God soon as he was
elected; ask why the Godly leader
fails now to wear a laurel crown, or fails

to show identification--a sign
like earth shaking, or blaze of comet star
trailing in sky above his very drive
toward Babylon; young, blonde, blue eyed now is

saved by the bell; no time to think, no time
for rebutted explanation, she picks
up her books and purse, she's out the door of
History, back inside her youth of now

Ryan Wilson

For a Dog

You'd wake us up—that shrill, insistent bark
Driving away whatever dreams had fogged
Our vision—and we'd rise in the true dark,

Wondering just what exactly, catalogued
By canine instinct under 'THREAT,' was there,
What jogger, cat, or dog it was that dogged

You from your drowse beside the easy chair
And summoned your yapped pandemonium.
Nine times in ten it was just empty air,

Some ghosted scent you sniffed. Dumb—you were dumb,
Like all dogs, snuffling up to snakes, afraid
Of mice. When we said 'come,' you wouldn't come;

You capered when commanded to play dead,
And when we wanted most to be alone
You'd offer up that imbecilic head

Until we crowned your pity with a bone.
Our lives took on the shape you spun from need,
The harried rondure of routine. You gone,

The house is quieter, and we've been freed
Forever from the never-ending chores
Your tail entailed, the scrubbing where you peed,

The hunting stain-removers down in stores.
What's hardest are the peaceful hours we wanted
So much when you were scratching up the doors

And howling at some phantom thing that haunted
The world without, some threat we couldn't see
That you were desperate to have confronted.

Now you're part of that present unity
Of absences the living move among,
In which what was, what will, and what can't be

Dance in a ring to a triumphant song
We don't have ears to hear, or heart to see,
Who sleep now perfectly, and much too long.

Ryan Wilson

In the Harvest Season

It's finished. Waiting's all that will remain.
The gossip now must go unverified.
Blue smoke from leaf-piles, smoldering like pride,
Hangs here, a ghost, a storm-cloud that can't rain.
Last night, the county's final weathervane
Fell in the high winds. Old roofs, stripped bare, preside.
Take down the ragged self you've crucified
And let the crows wing through the fields of grain.

The sagging fence will never stand up straight.
Whatever's not ripe now will never be.
That pain tormenting you will not abate,
And in the windows of vacated banks
You'll see yourself, passing by aimlessly.
You cannot change your life. Give up; give thanks.

CONTRIBUTORS' NOTES

Alan Berecka is a librarian at Del Mar College in Corpus Christi. His poems have appeared in *Ruminate, Penwood Review, Windhover,* and *Christian Century.* He has authored four collections of poems. His latest, *The Hamlet of Stittville,* is a collaboration with John Klossner, a boyhood friend and freelance cartoonist whose work has appeared in the *New Yorker* and other national weekly magazines. In 2017 Berecka was named Poet Laureate of Corpus Christi.

David Brunton wordsmithed his way in the career world of corporate communications with occasional side visits to poetry, recently published in his chapbook, *Footprints in the Dew*; there is a pastoral and spiritual thread in these works, woven into all the human disillusions of love and life that are only mended by God. Brunton currently teaches English at Lakeland Community College in Ohio as adjunct faculty.

William Bedford Clark is professor of English at Texas A&M University and has published widely in the field of American literature. His poetry has appeared in *Modern Age, the Sewanee Review,* and elsewhere. His poems have been collected in *Blue Norther* (Texas Review Press, 2010) and the chapbook *Ways And Means* (Caminada Bay Press, 2016).

David Craig has taught at Franciscan for 30 plus years, has published 25 books, large and small. (These keep him, for the most part, out of trouble.) He cannot account for anything, but would like to thank Jesus for being God and for rising from the dead. He would also like to thank his wife Linda and his children for putting up with him and his occasional silences.

Linda Craig is a stay at home maker of messes. Her tenacity in her study of the piano music of Bach and Beethoven is known only to her family and her teacher, Roberta Fedoush, and now, of course, to you. She enjoys finding things around the house to photograph, including her own artwork, growing green things outside and inside the house, adoring Jesus in the Holy Eucharist. And momming.

Sybil Pittman Estess was born in southern Mississippi and stayed there until she left for Baylor University in 1960. She married a fellow student, and achieved an M.A at the University of Kentucky. Her Ph.D. is from Syracuse University. She has five books of poems, two critical books, and a memoir to appear soon. She has been nominated twice for Poet Laureate of Texas and once came in second--when Paul Ruffin was granted the honor. She has also been nominated three times for TLS. Sybil lives in Houston.

John Finlay (1941-91) was born in Ozark, Alabama. His collections of verse and prose include *The Wide Porch and Other Poems* (1984), *Between the Gulfs* (1986), *The Salt of Exposure* (1988), *Mind and Blood: The Collected Poems of John Finlay*, and *Hermetic Light: Essays on the Gnostic Spirit in Modern Literature and Thought* (1994). An expanded two-volume edition of Finlay's collected verse and prose is forthcoming from Wiseblood Books.

Andrew Laurence Graney received his MFA in Creative Writing from Seattle Pacific University in the spring of 2018. He has work published or forthcoming in *The American Journal of Poetry, Redheaded Stepchild, Saint Katherine Review, Right Hand Pointing, Presence,* and elsewhere. He is from Wilmington, DE.

Kathleen Hart's collection *A Cut -and-Paste Country* (Franciscan University Press, 2016) was selected for the inaugural Jacopone da Todi Poetry Prize. Her work appears in *Glass: a Journal of Poetry, Red River Review,* and *Poetic Medicine.* Hart currently resides in Texas.

Janet McCann is an old Texas poet who taught at Texas A & M University from 1969-2016, is now Professor Emerita. She received an NEA Poetry Fellowship in 1089. She has co-edited anthologies with David Craig, and authored poetry books. Most recent poetry collection: *The Crone at the Casino* (Lamar University Press, 2014).

Paul McCann has had poems in numerous journals, *including Hawaii Pacific Review, Berkeley Poetry Review, Bayou Magazine.* His collection, *When the Wood is Green,* was published in 2014 by Slough Press. He is Professor of English at Del Mar College, and lives in Rockport, Texas with his family.

Leo Luke Marcello, (1945 – 2005). Leo's books of poetry include, *The Secret Proximity of Everywhere* (Blue Heron Press, 1994), *Blackrobe's Love Letters* (Xavier Review Press, 1994), *Silent Film* (Mellen Poetry Press, 1997), and *Nothing Grows in One Place Forever* (Time Being Books, 1998). He is also the author of *15 Days of Prayer with Saint Katharine Drexel* (Ligouri, 2002) and the editor of *Everything Comes to Light: A Festschrift for Joy Scantlebury* (The Cramers Press, 1993). His awards include the David Lloyd Kreeger Award in poetry as well as a Deep South Writers Award.

David Middleton is Poet in Residence Emeritus at Nicholls State University in Thibodaux, Louisiana. His collections of verse include *The Burning Fields* (1991), *Beyond the Chandeleurs* (1999), *The Habitual Peacefulness of Gruchy: Poems After Pictures by Jean-François Millet* (2005), and *The Fiddler of Driskill Hill* (2013). In 2006 Middleton won the Allen Tate Award for best poetry published in *The Sewanee Review* for 2005.

Kay Mullen's poems have been published in various journals and anthologies, including *Valparaiso Poetry Review, San Pedro River Review,* and *American Life in Poetry.* She has authored three books of poetry. Kay earned an MFA from the Rainier Writer Workshop at Pacific Lutheran University. She lives and teaches in Tacoma, Washington.

Stella Nesanovich is the author of two full-length poetry collections: *Vespers at Mount Angel* and *Colors of the River,* as well as four chapbooks of poems. Her poetry has appeared in many journals and magazines as well as over twenty anthologies. She is Professor Emerita of English from McNeese State University in Lake Charles, Louisiana.

Lois Roma-Deeley is the author of four full-length collections of poetry, most recently, *The Short List of Certainties*, and is a recent winner of the Jacopone da Todi Book Prize (Franciscan University Press). Roma-Deeley's poems have been featured in numerous literary journals and anthologies. She serves as Associate Editor of *Presence: A Journal of Catholic Poetry.*

Olympia Sibley earned her PhD in English Literature from Texas A&M University, and is a full-time faculty member at Blinn College. When she is not in the classroom, or chanting church services at the small Russian Orthodox Church of which her husband is the priest, or visiting her grandchildren, she enjoys spending time in her tree-house on 5 rural acres in Grimes County. Her poems have appeared in *Fjords*, *Rock & Sling*, and *Francis and Clare in Poetry*.

Chuck Taylor, mostly a Yankee raised in Texas, Minnesota, Illinois, and North Carolina, won the Austin Book Award. He worked Poets-in-the-Schools, operated a bookstore, owned a small press, and is the former Creative Writing Coordinator at Texas A&M. Taylor publishes prose, plays, and poetry; canoes Texas Hill Country spring-fed rivers; volunteers in politics; and does magic for children's birthday parties.

Ryan Wilson is the editor of *Literary Matters* and the author of *The Stranger World* (Measure Press, 2017), winner of the Donald Justice Poetry Prize. His work appears widely in periodicals such as *First Things*, *The Hopkins Review*, *The New Criterion*, *The Sewanee Review*, *The Yale Review*, and *Best American Poetry*. He teaches at The Catholic University of America.

Acknowledgements

Thanks to all the poets and editors who have allowed us to use work in *Catholic Things.* Alan Berecka's poems come from his collections, "Beatification" originally appeared in *Adanna Literary Journal* and was used in *The Hamlet of Stittville,* Tale Feathers Press 2017. "Momma Tried" appeared in *With Our Baggage,* Lamar University Press, 2013. David Brunton's poems come from his collection *Footprints in the Mist* (Piddiddle, 2017). William Bedford Clark's come from his collection *Ways and Means,* John Finlay's poems are printed by permission of his literary editor, David Middleton. Andrew Lawrence Graney's poem *Failing to Concentrate as I Try to Read, I Set the Book on my Desk and Close my Eyes* was in *Presence.* Kathleen Hart's poem "The Last Day" was in *Cut-and-Paste Country,* Franciscan University Press, 2015. Leo Luke Marcello's poem is published by permission of his brother, Chris Marcello. David Middleton's poems appeared in *The Anglican.* Janet McCann's poems are from her collection *The Crone at the Casino* (Lamar University Press, 2014). Paul McCann's poems are *from When the Wood is Green* (Slough Press, 2014). Ryan Wilson's poems are in his book *The Stranger World* (Measure Press, 2017); "For a Dog" was first published in *The Yale Review.*

www.ingramcontent.com/pod-product-compliance
Lightning Source LLC
Chambersburg PA
CBHW071224170626
46809CB00005BA/1930